SPACE SCIENCE

Earth's Moon

By Jennifer Lombardo

Published in 2024 by Cavendish Square Publishing, LLC
2544 Clinton Street Buffalo, NY 14224

Copyright © 2024 by Cavendish Square Publishing, LLC

First Edition

No part of this publication may be reproduced, stored in a retrieval system, or transmitted in any form or by any means—electronic, mechanical, photocopying, recording, or otherwise—without the prior permission of the copyright owner. Request for permission should be addressed to Permissions, Cavendish Square Publishing, 2544 Clinton Street Buffalo, NY 14224. Tel (877) 980-4450; fax (877) 980-4454.

Website: cavendishsq.com

This publication represents the opinions and views of the author based on their personal experience, knowledge, and research. The information in this book serves as a general guide only. The author and publisher have used their best efforts in preparing this book and disclaim liability rising directly or indirectly from the use and application of this book.

All websites were available and accurate when this book was sent to press.

Library of Congress Cataloging-in-Publication Data

Names: Lombardo, Jennifer, author.
Title: Earth's moon / [Jennifer Lombardo].
Description: Buffalo, NY : Cavendish Square Publishing, [2024] | Series: The inside guide: space science | Includes bibliographical references and index.
Identifiers: LCCN 2023025192 | ISBN 9781502670137 (library binding) | ISBN 9781502670120 (paperback) | ISBN 9781502670144 (ebook)
Subjects: LCSH: Moon–Juvenile literature.
Classification: LCC QB582 .L66 2024 | DDC 523.3–dc23/eng20230718
LC record available at https://lccn.loc.gov/2023025192

Editor: Jennifer Lombardo
Copyeditor: Jill Keppeler
Designer: Deanna Lepovich

The photographs in this book are used by permission and through the courtesy of: Cover 24K-Production/Shutterstock.com; p. 4 Rolling Stones/Shutterstock.com; p. 6 SN VFX/Shutterstock.com; p. 7 vovan/Shutterstock.com; p. 9 mountain beetle/Shutterstock.com; p. 10 jules2000/Shutterstock.com; p. 12 Vector Tradition/Shutterstock.com; p. 13 Michael Andrew Just/Shutterstock.com; p. 15 (main) Elena11/Shutterstock.com; p. 15 (inset) Mickicev Atelje/Shutterstock.com; p. 16 Knoph Photography/Shutterstock.com; p. 18 photos4ya/Shutterstock.com; p. 19 Designua/Shutterstock.com; p. 20 NASA; p. 22 Yvonne Baur/Shutterstock.com; p. 25 HelenField/Shutterstock.com; p. 27 Willyam Bradberry/Shutterstock.com; p. 28 (top) Sarah Holmlund/Shutterstock.com; p. 28 (bottom) 010110010101101/Shutterstock.com; p. 29 (top) stylefoto24/Shutterstock.com; p. 29 (bottom) Zoomik/Shutterstock.com.

Some of the images in this book illustrate individuals who are models. The depictions do not imply actual situations or events.

CPSIA compliance information: Batch #CWCSQ24: For further information contact Cavendish Square Publishing LLC at 1-877-980-4450.

Printed in the United States of America

CONTENTS

Chapter One: 5
   Moon Myths

Chapter Two: 11
   Our Natural Satellite

Chapter Three: 17
   A Helpful Partner

Chapter Four: 23
   Where Did It Come From?

Think About It! 28

Glossary 30

Find Out More 31

Index 32

A Chinese myth says a woman named Chang'e lives on the moon with her pet rabbit.

MOON MYTHS

Chapter One

Humans haven't always known what the moon was, but they have always been able to see it. Early civilizations made up myths, or stories, to explain where the moon came from and why it went through **phases** each month. For example, a story from Siberia, Russia, says that a huge monster named Alklha eats the moon every month. The dark spots we see are its tooth marks. It nibbles the moon away bit by bit, but then it throws up the pieces until the moon is full again.

Good Guesses

In the past, before things such as telescopes and spacecraft were invented, people could only guess at what the moon was and how it affected our planet. Sometimes these guesses were right. Some of the earliest humans used the moon and its phases to keep track of time. Noting its position in the sky relative to the position of the stars

Fast Fact

Professor Anthony Aveni of Colgate University in Hamilton, New York, is a founder of the field of archaeoastronomy. This is a combination of archaeology, the study of the past, and astronomy, the study of space.

5

The word "month" comes from an Old English word that is related to "moon." In the past, a month was the time period from one new moon to the next.

Fast Fact
Many Western **cultures** talk about seeing a man in the moon. In most Eastern cultures, people see a rabbit, not a man.

also helped them keep track of things such as when it was time to plant and harvest crops.

The ancient Greeks developed an even better understanding of the moon. A Greek astronomer named Aristarchus used math to figure out that the moon

Without a telescope, people can't see the craters on the moon. The dark spots we see are a dark kind of rock called basalt.

and the sun only appear to be the same size in the sky because the sun is much farther away from Earth. Then, when the telescope was invented in 1608, people saw the moon in detail for the first time. The ancient Greeks thought it was smooth, but Galileo Galilei realized that it's actually covered in craters.

Getting It Wrong

Other times, people's guesses were wrong. Many ancient people blamed the moon for odd things, real

Fast Fact

In England in the 1700s, people who had committed murder during a full moon were sometimes given less prison time if they blamed the moon for their actions.

A TASTY MOON

In 1546, a man named John Heywood wrote a book of **proverbs**, many of which are still used today. One of the proverbs was a joke about the moon being made of green cheese. People have used this joke to talk about someone who will believe anything you tell them.

Although no one actually believes the moon is made of cheese, there are many stories about it. For example, one Serbian fairy tale involves a wolf and a fox. The fox convinces the wolf not to eat it by telling it that there's a huge cheese wheel at the bottom of a nearby pond. The wolf tries to drink the pond to get to the "cheese" (the moon's reflection) and bursts.

or imaginary, that happened at night. For example, sleepwalking, werewolves, and mental illness were all associated with the moon. The Roman goddess of the moon was named Luna; the words "lunacy" and "lunatic," which are unkind words used to talk about mental illness, came from her name. Even ancient doctors were convinced that the moon made people mentally ill. Today, many people still believe that people act strangely when the moon is full.

Another thing many early peoples believed is that the moon controls **fertility**. This is because one cycle of the moon—where it goes from full to new and back to full again—is about the same length as a **menstrual** cycle for many people assigned (said to be)

Astronomy is the scientific study of space. Astrology, shown here, is the use of the moon, stars, planets, and other bodies to predict the future or explain why people behave the way they do. It isn't a real science.

female at birth. This is one reason why many ancient civilizations believed the moon was a woman or was controlled by a goddess.

Our moon is the fifth largest moon in the solar system. It's about one-fourth the size of Earth.

OUR NATURAL SATELLITE

Chapter Two

Scientists define a moon as an object that orbits a planet. They don't take size into account, so a moon could be huge or tiny. A planet can also have more than one moon. In fact, in our solar system, Earth is unusual because it's the only planet with one moon!

Revolution and Rotation

The way the moon looks in the sky depends on where it is in its orbit and rotation. The moon's orbit isn't a perfect circle, so there are certain times of the month when it's closer to Earth, and other times when it's farther away. The point where it's closest to the planet is called perigee, and the point where it's farthest away is called apogee.

While the moon is orbiting Earth, it's also rotating on its **axis**. However, the moon rotates much slower than Earth does. It takes 24 hours for Earth to rotate on its axis; this is why a day is 24 hours long. Meanwhile, the moon's "day" is about 27 Earth days long.

Fast Fact
A satellite is something that orbits a heavenly body. Satellites can be natural, such as a moon or a comet, or they can be man-made. Some man-made satelittes help us use our phones and watch TV.

Mercury
0

Pluto
(dwarf planet)
5

Venus
0

Neptune
14

Number of Moons

Earth
1

Saturn
124

Uranus
27

Mars
2

Jupiter
95

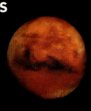

This picture shows the number of moons each planet in our solar system has, as well as Pluto's moons.

When the moon is full and at perigee, it looks up to 17 percent bigger and 30 percent brighter than at other times of the year. We call this a "supermoon."

Additionally, it takes as much time for the moon to complete one revolution around Earth as it does to complete one rotation. Because of these two things, the moon doesn't look like it's rotating at all. From Earth, we can only

Fast Fact

The moon is about 1,080 miles (1,740 kilometers) across. That's about the same distance as a road trip from Orlando, Florida, to New York City.

UNDERSTANDING ECLIPSES

An eclipse happens when the moon, the sun, and Earth all line up. A solar eclipse is when the moon passes between Earth and the sun, and a lunar eclipse is when Earth passes between the moon and the sun.

There are two kinds of lunar eclipses we can see well. The first is a total eclipse. This is when Earth completely blocks the light of the sun from reaching the moon. The second is a partial eclipse. This is when not all the light is blocked, so some part of the moon can still be seen throughout the whole eclipse.

ever see one side of the moon. The other side, which we call the "far side" or "dark side," is always facing away from us. This is called "tidal locking."

Fast Fact

Outside our solar system, many planets are tidally locked with their star. If Earth were tidally locked to the sun, it would always be daytime on one side of the planet and always nighttime on the other!

It's Just a Phase

As the moon is orbiting Earth, Earth is orbiting the sun—and taking the moon with it. This is why the moon goes through monthly phases. The moon has no light of its own. When we see it lit up, it's because the sun's light is reflecting off it. When the near side of the moon is lit up, we see a full moon. When its far side is lit up, we see a new moon. The phases in between happen as the moon continues its rotation and revolution.

The phases of the moon, in order, are new moon, waxing crescent, first quarter, waxing gibbous, full moon, waning gibbous, third or last quarter, and waning crescent. It takes about a month for it to pass through all these phases.

This picture shows a beach at low tide.

A HELPFUL PARTNER

Chapter Three

The moon isn't just a decoration in the sky. It's also been an important part of maintaining life on Earth. One of the most noticeable ways it does this is through the tides. The moon's gravity pulls at Earth, causing the water in the oceans to bulge out on the sides closest to and farthest from the moon. This creates what we call "high tide." Low tide is the opposite—lower water levels.

Life as We Know It

Scientists believe life couldn't exist on Earth if the planet wasn't always changing. For example, the tides might not seem that important, but they're a big part of keeping coastal life alive. If coastal life died out, other plants and animals that rely on it would also die out. The tides are also responsible for helping to move the planet's heat around. Without the oceans' tidal flow, the equator would likely be much hotter and

Fast Fact
We talk about the tide going in and out, but in reality, the tidal bulges stay in the same spot. As Earth rotates, certain parts of the land pass through the bulges at high tide and move away from them at low tide.

17

When the tide goes out, it leaves behind tide pools, where many coastal plants and animals thrive.

the poles much colder than they are now.

The moon is also partially responsible for keeping Earth **stable**.

Fast Fact

Many nocturnal animals need the moon's reflected light to see their prey at night. Without the moon, animals such as owls, raccoons, and foxes would have trouble finding food and might starve.

Earth is tilted on its axis, and the moon's gravity pulls on the planet to keep that tilt at about 23.5 degrees all the time. The seasons change because Earth moves around the sun but its tilt always stays the same. Without the moon's gravity, it's possible that Earth would swing back and forth as it rotates. We might go from periods of time without any tilt at all to periods with a very large tilt. Imagine going outside every day not knowing if you

It's summer in whichever hemisphere, or half of the planet, is tilted toward the sun. It's winter in the hemisphere that's tilted away from the sun.

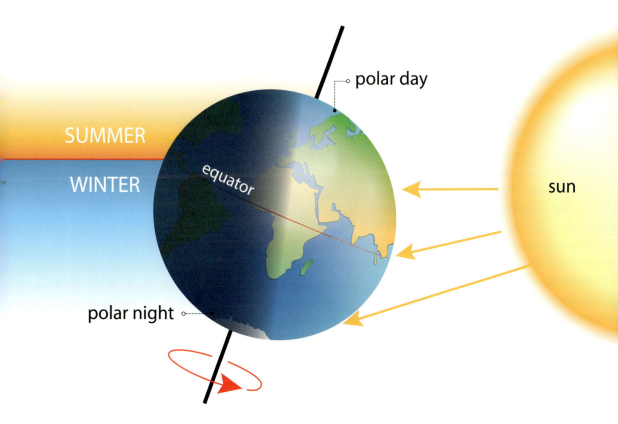

CALCULATING THE RECESSION RATE

Astronomer Edmond Halley was the first person to guess that the moon was moving away from the planet. He figured this out in 1695 by looking at historical records of eclipses that happened in ancient times. However, no one could prove that he was right until humans went to space in the 1960s and 1970s.

When astronauts landed on the moon, they set up reflecting panels facing Earth. Scientists on Earth aimed laser beams at the panels and kept track of how long it took the light to bounce back to the planet. As this amount of time got a little bit longer each year, scientists were able to figure out that Halley's theory, or idea, had been right.

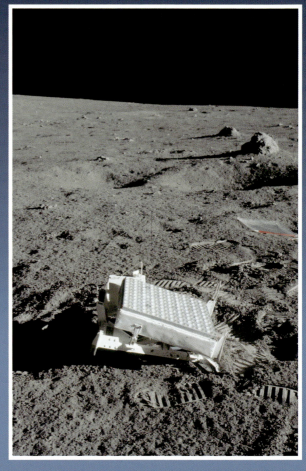

This picture shows one of the reflecting panels that was placed on the moon in 1971.

were stepping into a heat wave or an ice age!

Slowing Down

The moon stays in Earth's orbit because Earth's gravity pulls it in. However, the moon has its own gravity and is pulling right back. The tides created by this pull cause **drag** on Earth, which slows the planet's rotation down. This weakens its pull on the moon, causing the moon to recede, or move away. Right now, the moon is about 238,800 miles (384,400 km) from Earth. About 30 Earths could fit in the space between the Earth and the moon. Every year, the moon moves 1.5 inches (3.8 cm) farther away. This is called its recession rate—how much it recedes in a year.

Ever since the moon was formed, it's been receding from Earth. However, it hasn't always been moving away as fast as it is now. Earth has gone through many changes since its formation. Over billions of years, its landmasses have moved, changing the size and depth of the oceans. This, in turn, changed the amount of tidal drag, speeding up the moon's recession rate as time went on.

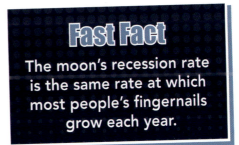

Fast Fact
The moon's recession rate is the same rate at which most people's fingernails grow each year.

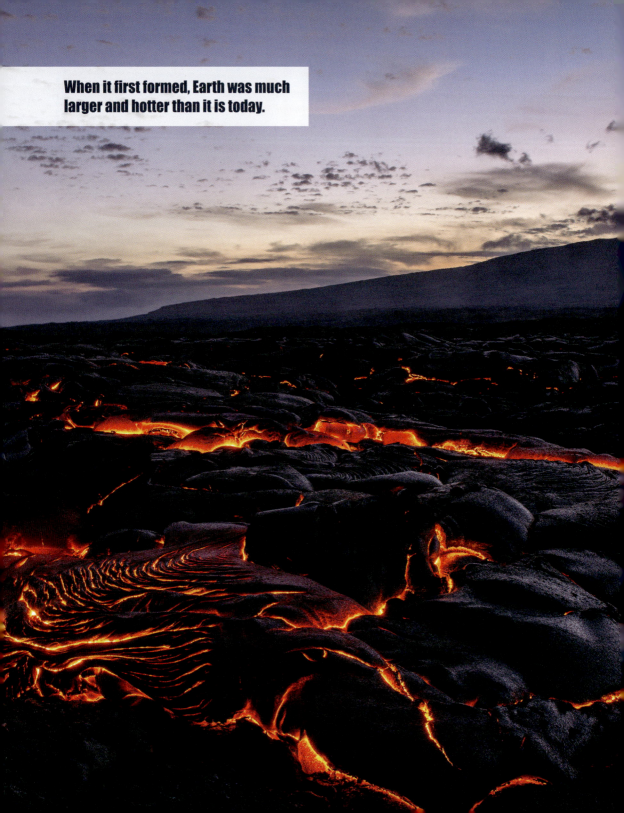

When it first formed, Earth was much larger and hotter than it is today.

WHERE DID IT COME FROM?

Chapter Four

It's clear that the moon is an important part of keeping plants and animals alive. However, it may also have helped create life on Earth in the first place. Scientists believe that billions of years ago, when Earth first formed, the planet was much larger than it is today. It was also much hotter—so hot, in fact, that it would be impossible for anything to survive.

Understanding the Impact

When Earth first formed, it was very hot. Before it had a chance to cool to the point where solid land would form, a Mars-sized object hit it with enough force to break off part of it. Scientists call this object "Theia," which is the name of the mother of the goddess of the moon in Greek mythology.

Liquid rock and dust from both Earth and Theia flew into space. Over

> **Fast Fact**
> Like Earth, the moon has a molten, or hot liquid, core. This caused volcanoes to erupt on the moon for more than 1 billion years after it first formed.

23

THREE THEORIES

There are three main theories about where the moon came from. The co-formation theory says the moon and Earth formed near each other at the same time from the same matter. The capture theory says the moon traveled through the solar system and was pulled into Earth's orbit when it got too close.

The third theory is called the **impact** theory. This is the one that talks about Theia hitting Earth. It has the most evidence, or facts, to back it up, so it's been the most commonly accepted theory since the mid-1970s. However, there are still many questions left unanswered about where the moon came from.

Fast Fact
The capture theory is unlikely to be true because Earth isn't big enough to slowly pull something the size of the moon into its orbit. If the moon came from somewhere else, it would have been moving fast enough to smash into the planet.

time, gravity pulled these pieces into a ball, which cooled to become the moon. This may explain why our moon is so much bigger than most other moons in the solar system: It had more material to form from.

This theory explains why the moon and Earth are made up of mostly—but not all—the same material.

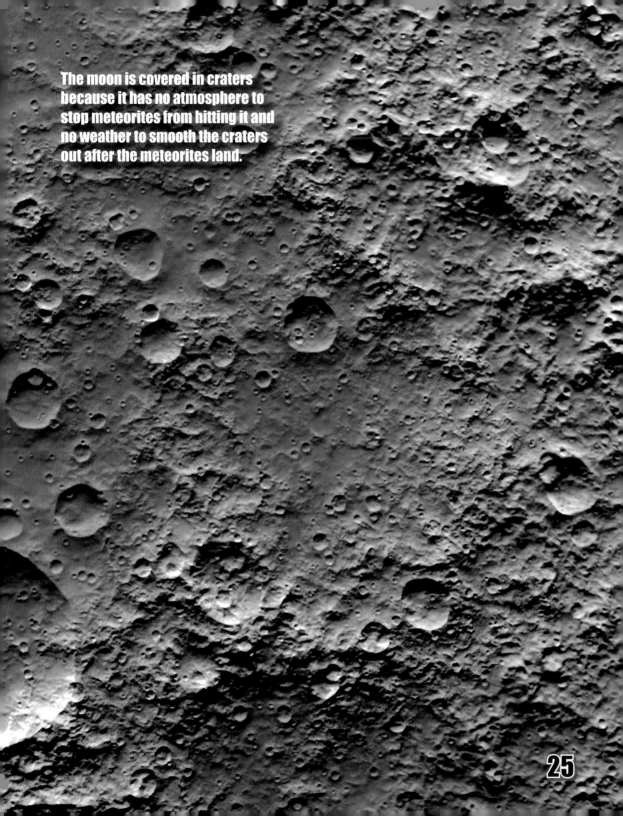

The moon is covered in craters because it has no atmosphere to stop meteorites from hitting it and no weather to smooth the craters out after the meteorites land.

If they formed at the same time, they'd be exactly the same; if Earth pulled the moon into its orbit from far away, they'd be completely different.

Making Changes

Scientists believe that the force of the impact made Earth spin much faster, giving it 12-hour days. Within a few thousand years, the Earth had cooled to a point where oceans could form. About 700 million years after that, life began to emerge, or develop. Some scientists believe the tides played a big part in that. Because the tides move heat from the equator to the poles, it's likely they helped balance out the planet's climate to a point where it was the right temperature for living things.

> **Fast Fact**
> A 12-hour day on Earth would create a high tide once every 6 hours. With our 24-hour day, high tide happens once every 12 hours.

The tides may also have helped make large parts of Earth very salty. Huge waves pulled by a close moon would have traveled for miles inland at high tide, leaving behind salt and pools of water at low tide. The basic building blocks of life, which are called nucleic acids, need this kind of environment to form.

Many scientists believe that without this early flooding, it would have been difficult or impossible for life to form on Earth. As the moon moved away and the tides became less intense, or powerful, the planet became more comfortable for different types of life, leading to **diversity** in plants and animals.

As you can see, the moon is more than just a far-off object in space. It's an important part of life on Earth!

When the moon finished forming, it was much closer to Earth than it is now, so the tides it created would have been much more powerful.

THINK ABOUT IT!

1. Why do you think the moon has been so strongly linked to things many people find scary?

2. What would the moon look like to us if it weren't tidally locked?

3. How do you think coastal life would be affected if there were no tides?

4. What do you think Earth would be like today if the impact with Theia had never happened?

GLOSSARY

axis: An imaginary line around which an object rotates.

culture: The customs and ways of life of a group of people.

diversity: Being made up of different things.

drag: A force that slows down motion.

fertility: The ability to reproduce.

impact: The action of one thing hitting another.

menstrual: Relating to menstruation, or the monthly discharge of blood and tissue from the uterus—a reproductive organ in most people assigned female at birth (AFAB). This discharge is also known as a period.

phase: A particular appearance or state in a repeating series of changes.

predict: To figure out in advance.

proverb: A short, popular saying.

stable: Not easily changed or affected.

thrive: To grow and flourish.

FIND OUT MORE

Books
Buxner, Sanlyn, Georgiana Kramer, Palema L. Gay, and Dawn Cooper. *The Moon*. New York, NY: DK, 2022.

Rocco, John. *How We Got to the Moon: The People, Technology, and Daring Feats of Science Behind Humanity's Greatest Adventure*. New York, NY: Crown Books, 2020.

Sommer, Nathan. *The Moon*. Minneapolis, MN: Bellwether Media, 2019.

Websites

Kiddle: Moon Facts for Kids
kids.kiddle.co/Moon
Check out some cool pictures of the moon, moon rocks, and astronauts.

NASA Space Place: Moon
spaceplace.nasa.gov/search/moon
Read facts and do activities to learn more about the moon.

Planets for Kids: The Moon
www.planetsforkids.org/moon-moon.html
Learn more interesting information about our moon.

Publisher's note to educators and parents: Our editors have carefully reviewed these websites to ensure that they are suitable for students. Many websites change frequently, however, and we cannot guarantee that a site's future contents will continue to meet our high standards of quality and educational value. Be advised that students should be closely supervised whenever they access the internet.

INDEX

A
Alklha, 5
apogee, 11
archaeoastronomy, 5
Aristarchus, 6
astronauts, 20
Aveni, Anthony, 5
axis, 11, 19

B
basalt, 7

C
Chang'e, 4
craters, 7, 25

E
Earth, 7, 10, 11, 12, 13, 14, 17, 18, 19, 20, 21, 22, 23, 24, 26, 27
eclipses, 14, 20

F
full moon, 13, 14, 15

G
Galileo Galilei, 7
gravity, 17, 19, 21, 24
Greeks, 6, 7

H
Halley, Edmond, 20
Heywood, John, 8

J
Jupiter, 12

L
Luna, 8

M
Mars, 12
Mercury, 12
myths, 4, 5

N
Neptune, 12
new moon, 6, 14, 15

P
perigee, 11, 13
phases, 5, 14, 15
Pluto, 12

R
recession rate, 20, 21
Russia, 5

S
satellite, 11
Saturn, 12
sun, 7, 14

T
telescopes, 5, 7
Theia, 23, 24
tides, 16, 17, 18, 21, 26, 27

U
Uranus, 12

V
Venus, 12